SCHIRMER'S LIBRARY
OF MUSICAL CLASSICS

WOLFGANG AMADEUS MOZART

Concertos

For the Piano

Critically Revised, Fingered, and
the Orchestral Accompaniments
Arranged for a Second Piano by

FRANZ KULLAK

AND OTHERS

G. SCHIRMER, Inc.

DISTRIBUTED BY

HAL•LEONARD®
CORPORATION

7777 W. BLUEMOUND RD. P.O. BOX 13819 MILWAUKEE, WI 53213

PREFACE

The present edition of Mozart's Piano Concerto in A major is the result of a complete arrangement of the orchestral score, with the addition of some marks of dynamics, fingering, and phrasing.   The basis of the text is the full score in Breitkopf and Härtel's complete edition of Mozart's works. The editor has compared his work with the editions of Ruthardt, Lachner, Mertke, and Reinhold.   A very few slight errors, such as misprints or omissions, have been corrected.

As to the *legato* marks, it should be remembered that in Mozart's time these marks, originating in the bowing for the violin, did not always carry with them the implication that the last note under the curved line is to be "phrased", or played *staccato*, as is the case at present.   The player should accordingly be guided to a great extent by his musical sense when these curved lines end with a measure, especially on a short note.   Frequently the musical idea requires the continuation of the *legato* over to the following note.   Mozart's own use of the word *legato* for a long passage has been exchanged for the modern curved line.

The player will, of course, use his own fingering; but it is hoped that the few suggestions for fingering may prove helpful.

Mozart's own catalogue shows that this concerto was written (*i.e.*, probably, finished) March 2, 1786.   It seems to have been begun about the 3rd of the preceding month.   It was composed for one of three subscription concerts given that spring and was probably played by Mozart himself at one of these concerts.   It was known as Op. 82, No. 5, or— in Köchel's catalogue as number 488.   It was scored for strings, one flute, two clarinets, two bassoons, and two horns.   The abbreviations for these instruments used in the text are as follows: Str. (Strings), Cl. (Clarinet), Fl. (Flute), Bsn. (Bassoon), Hn. (Horn), and Ww. (Woodwind).

The editor considers anything approaching the modern use of the damper pedal to be entirely foreign to the Mozart idiom; but it is known that it was customary in Mozart's

time in playing passages like the following: to sustain the first note of

the group with the finger throughout the entire group; this suggests that in modern playing a slight touch of the pedal in such cases would not be objectionable.   The pedal, if used at all, should be used very sparingly.   However, in the case of the second piano, representing as it does the orchestra, its use is recommended, suggesting to some degree the greater sonority of the orchestra.

Mozart followed the custom of his time by opening the concerto with an extended orchestral part.   This is interesting when played by the orchestra, followed by the piano solo, because of the contrasting tone quality; but when played by one piano followed by another piano largely repeating what the first piano has just played, the effect, at least to modern ears, is wearisome.   So it is suggested that in public performance with two pianos, all of this orchestral part at the beginning after the seventeenth measure be omitted except the five measures immediately preceding the entrance of the Solo.

Mozart's own Cadenza in the first movement has been retained.   If the player wishes something more elaborate, there are cadenzas written by Mertke, Linder, Reinecke, Busoni, and others, that are available.

FRANCIS L. YORK

39032

Concerto in A major
for Piano and Orchestra
[K. 488]

Edited and orchestra score arranged for Piano II by
Francis L. York

Wolfgang Amadeus Mozart

I

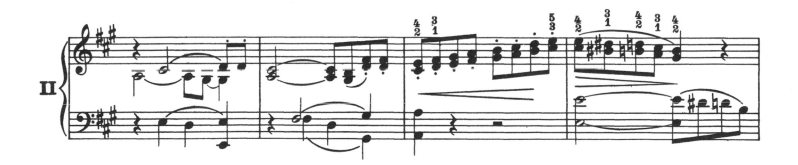

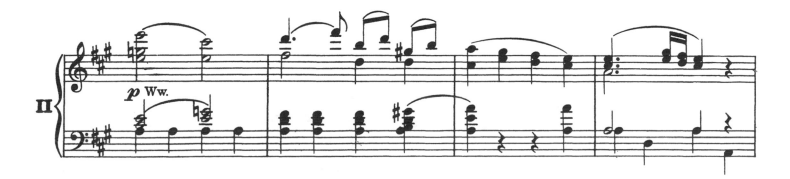

39032 c

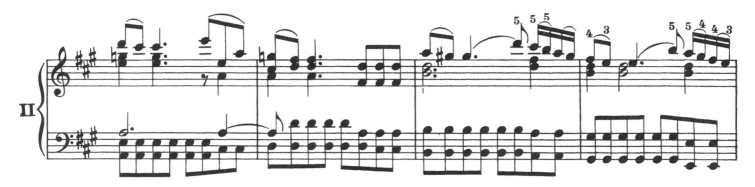

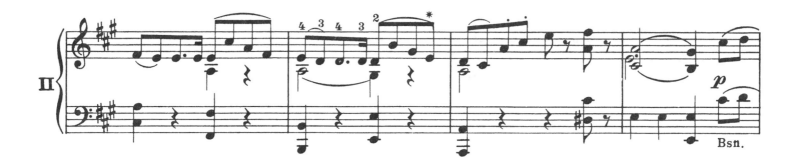

*Some editions have d.

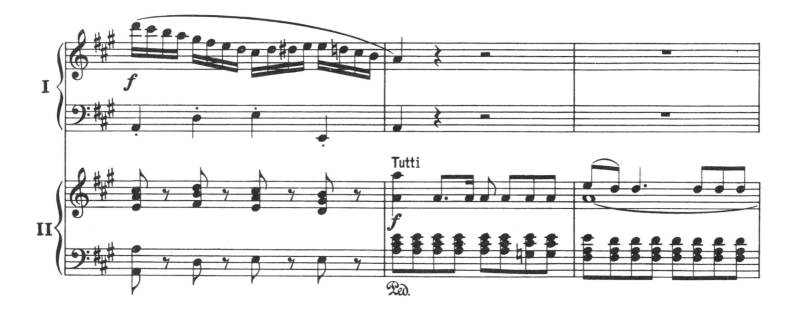

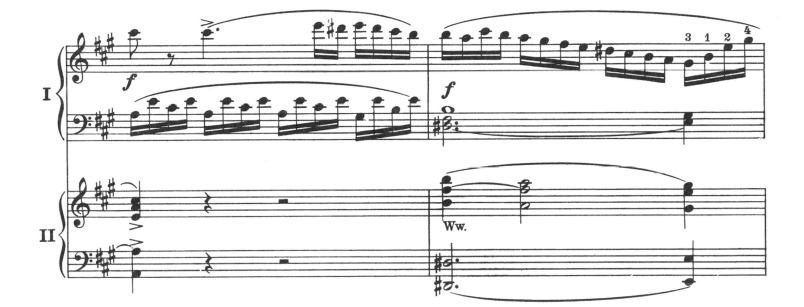

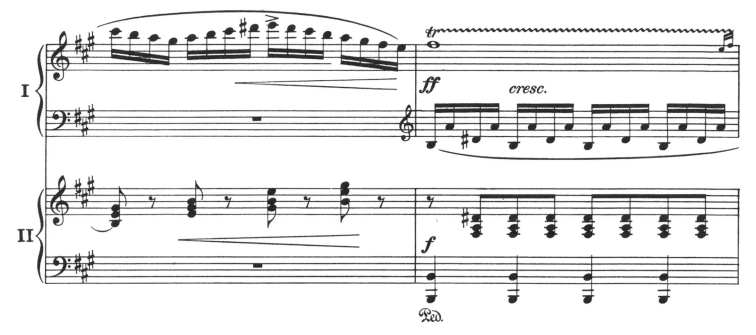

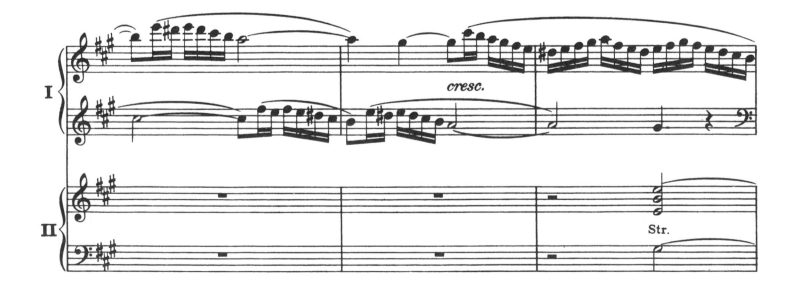

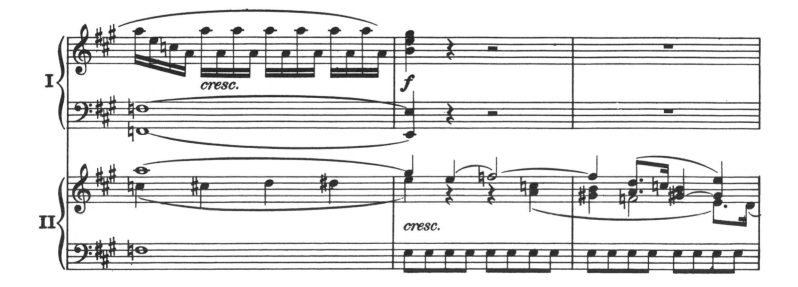

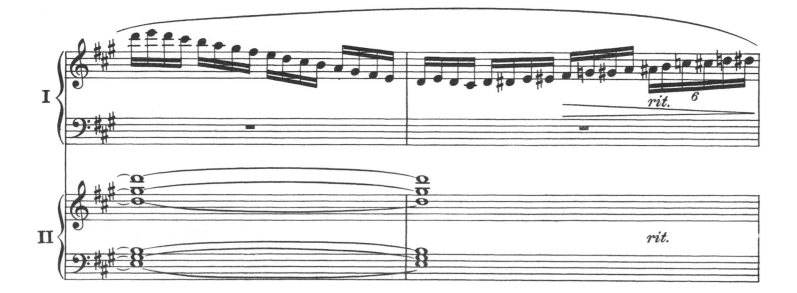

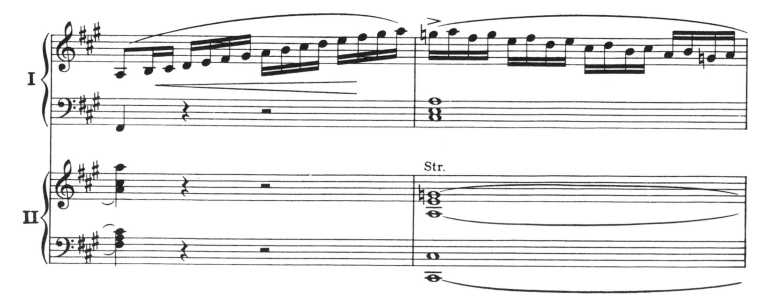

39032

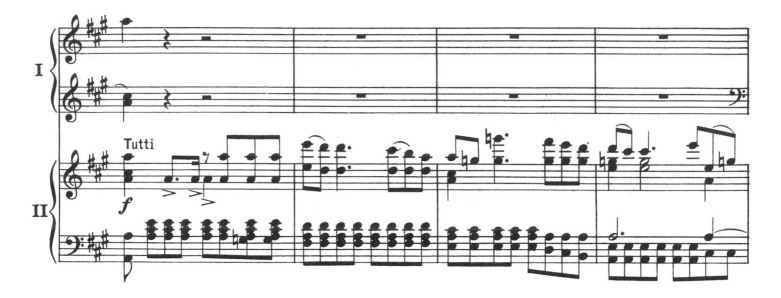

II

*Mozart's autograph MS. reads Adagio.

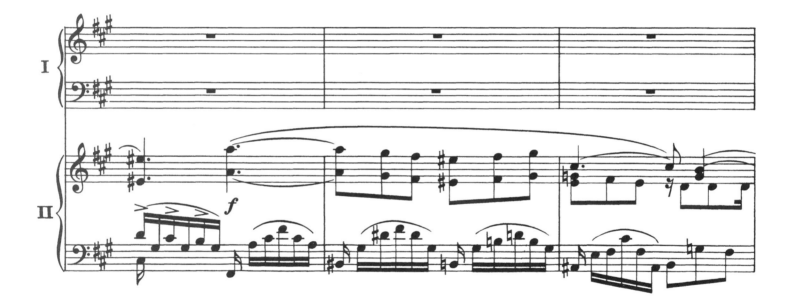

III

*Mozart's autograph MS. reads Allegro assai.

39032

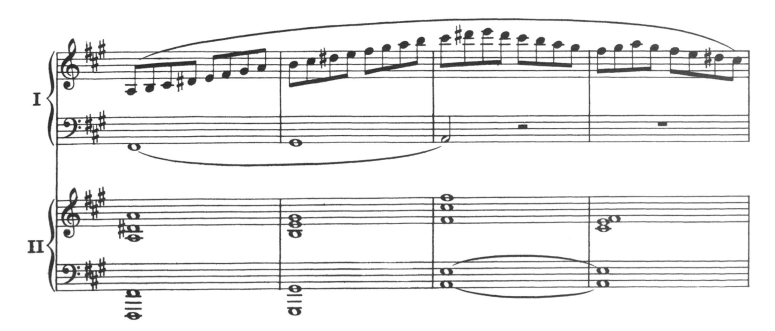

39032

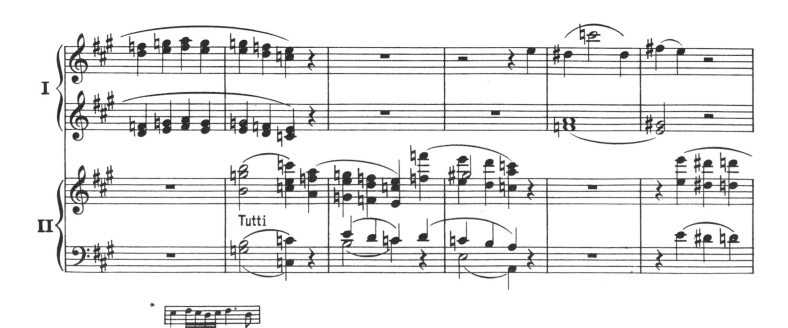

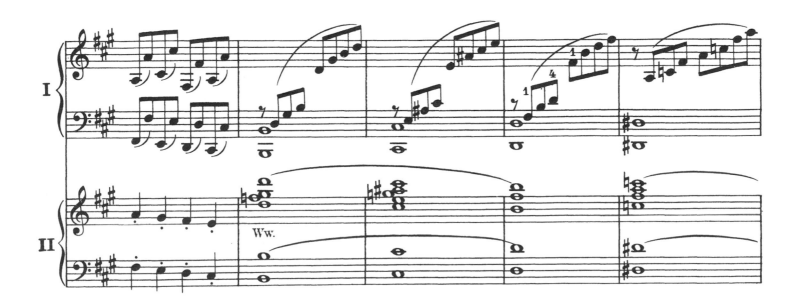

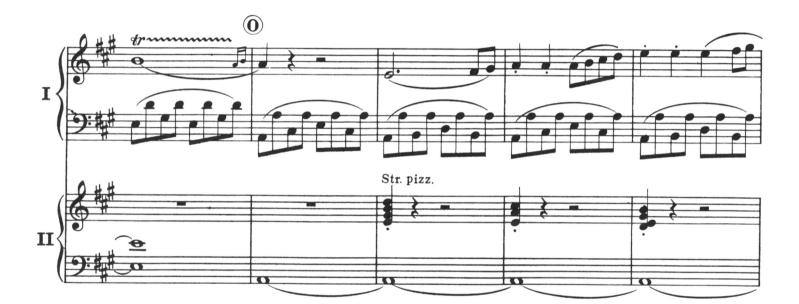

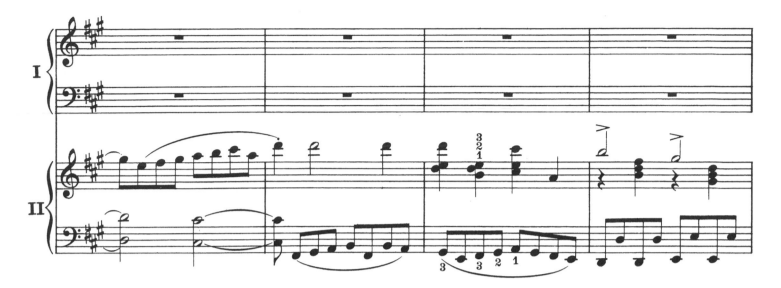

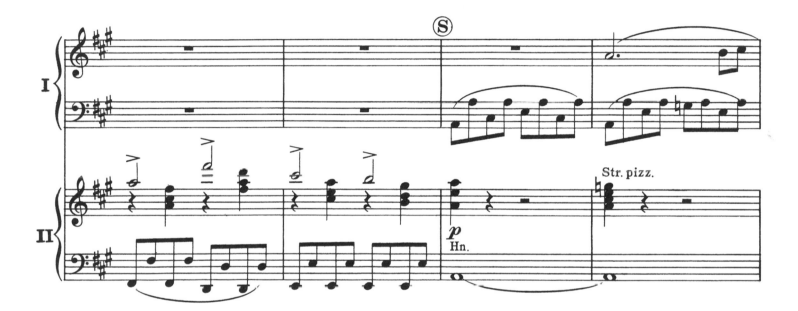

poco marcato il canto